ULTIMATE TRIVIA CHALLENGE

AWESOME ANIMAL TRIVIA

By Lucy Rauker

Gareth Stevens
Publishing

Please visit our website, www.garethstevens.com. For a free color catalog of all our high-quality books, call toll free 1-800-542-2595 or fax 1-877-542-2596.

Library of Congress Cataloging-in-Publication Data

Rauker, Lucy.
Awesome animal trivia / by Lucy Rauker.
 p. cm. — (Ultimate trivia challenge)
Includes index.
ISBN 978-1-4339-8289-7 (pbk.)
ISBN 978-1-4339-8290-3 (6-pack)
ISBN 978-1-4339-8288-0 (library binding)
1. Animals—Juvenile literature. 2. Animals—Miscellanea—Juvenile literature. I. Title.
QL49.R38 2014
590—dc23

First Edition

Published in 2014 by
Gareth Stevens Publishing
111 East 14th Street, Suite 349
New York, NY 10003

Copyright © 2014 Gareth Stevens Publishing

Designer: Andrea Davison-Bartolotta
Editor: Greg Roza

Photo credits: Cover, p. 1 (giraffe) Anky/Shutterstock.com, (penguins) Jan Martin Will/Shutterstock.com, (horses) Eduard Kyslynskyy/Shutterstock.com; p. 4 glyph/Shutterstock.com; p. 5 (whale, jellyfish, beaver, alligator, bird, bullfrog) iStockphoto/Thinkstock, (giraffe, elephants) Digital Vision/Thinkstock, (chimps, crab, dragonfly, beetle) Stockbyte/Thinkstock, (ostriches, treefrog, iguana, tiger) Photodisc/Thinkstock, (fish, clownfish, squid, macaw, cows) Comstock/Thinkstock, (shark) Hemera/Thinkstock, (polar bear) Design Pics/Thinkstock; p. 6 Mark Carwardine/Peter Arnold/Getty Images; pp. 7, 12 (top), 18, 24, 29 (both) iStockphoto/Thinkstock; p. 8 Joel Shawn/Shutterstock.com; p. 9 © Dave Wilkie/iStockphoto.com; p. 10 Cameramannz/Shutterstock.com; p. 11 (main image) Brian Lasenby/Shutterstock.com; p. 11 (inset) John Cancalosi/Peter Arnold/Getty Images; p. 12 (bottom) Photos.com/Thinkstock; p. 13 Nature Images/UIG/Getty Images; p. 14 Last Refuge/Robert Harding World Imagery/Getty Images; p. 15 Frank Greenaway/Dorling Kindersley/Getty Images; p. 16 Rodger Klein/WaterFrame/Getty Images; p. 17 Teguh Tirtaputra/Shutterstock.com; p. 19 Thomas Marent/Visuals Unlimited/Getty Images; p. 20 (top) Sue Robinson/Shutterstock.com; p. 20 (bottom) Cheryl Ann Quigley/Shutterstock.com; p. 21 Martin Harvey/Gallo Images; p. 22 Ronaldo Schemidt/AFP/Getty Images; p. 23 Berndt Fischer/Oxford Scientific/Getty Images; p. 25 Pat Gaines/Flickr/Getty Images; p. 26 Dorling Kindersley/Getty Images; p. 27 © Paul Whillock/iStockphoto.com; p. 28 NYPL/Science Source/Photo Researchers/Getty Images.

Printed in the United States of America

CPSIA compliance information: Batch #CS13GS: For further information contact Gareth Stevens, New York, New York at 1-800-542-2595.

CONTENTS

Words in the glossary appear in **bold** type the first time they are used in the text.

THAT'S A LOT OF ANIMALS!

There are so many animal species, or kinds, on Earth that scientists can't be sure how many there actually are. So far, scientists have identified about 1.25 million animal species, but some think there could be 30 million! New species are discovered every year.

With that many animals on the planet, it's no wonder that there are so many interesting things to say about them. From the planet's largest animal to the loudest, there's a lot of awesome animal trivia.

GIANT ANIMALS

What is the largest animal on Earth?

Blue whales are truly giant. They can grow close to 100 feet (30 m) long. The largest blue whales weigh more than 150 tons (136 mt). That's about the same as 30 school buses!

BONUS TRIVIA

Scientists think the blue whale is probably the biggest animal ever to live on Earth—and that includes the dinosaurs!

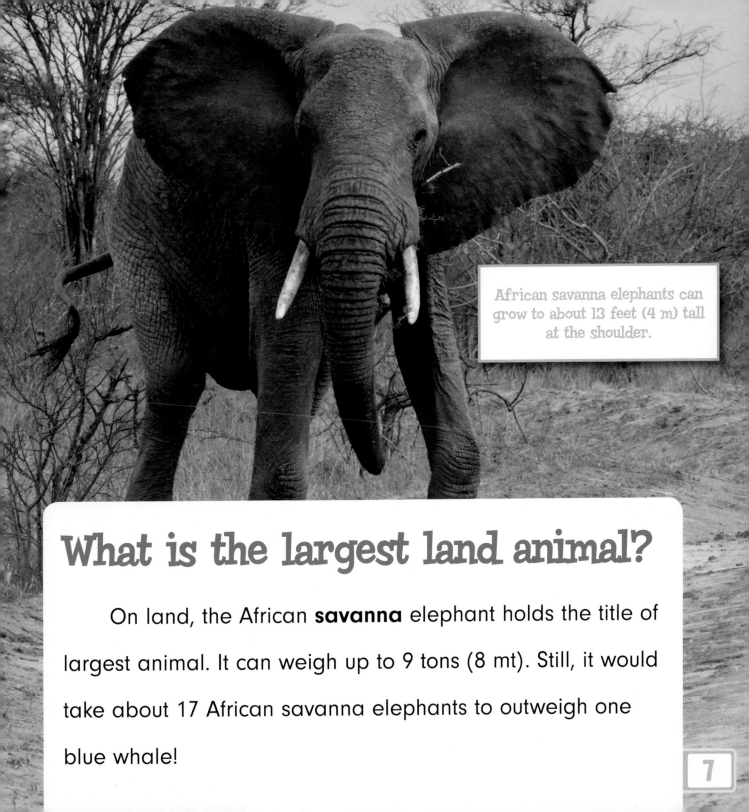

African savanna elephants can grow to about 13 feet (4 m) tall at the shoulder.

What is the largest land animal?

On land, the African **savanna** elephant holds the title of largest animal. It can weigh up to 9 tons (8 mt). Still, it would take about 17 African savanna elephants to outweigh one blue whale!

Which animal has the highest blood pressure?

Blood pressure is the force of blood pushing against the walls of the **blood vessels**. The animal with the highest blood pressure is the giraffe. That's because their heart needs to pump blood up to their head—a length of about 6 feet (1.8 m)!

BONUS TRIVIA

A giraffe's blood pressure is twice that of a person's.

Why is the giraffe's tongue blue?

Giraffes might have the longest neck in the animal kingdom, but their tongue is pretty long, too—18 to 20 inches (46 to 51 cm) long! A giraffe's tongue is a bluish color. This keeps it from getting sunburned!

Giraffes spend much of their time sticking out their long tongue to reach tasty grass and leaves, so it gets a lot of sun.

LEAPING LIZARDS!

Which animal only needs to breathe once an hour?

The tuatara lizard of New Zealand can live about 80 years. The tuatara's body processes are very slow. They don't finish growing until they're about 30 years old. If it needs to, this lizard can go a whole hour on a single breath.

BONUS TRIVIA

Tuataras have a third eye under the skin of their forehead that senses light.

Horned lizards live from Southern Canada down to Guatemala.

Which animal can shoot blood from its eyes?

The horned lizard is covered with short **spines**. When an animal tries to eat it, this lizard can suck in air and grow to twice its normal size. This isn't the weirdest way it stays safe. Some horned lizards can also shoot blood out of their eyes!

GOING BUGGY!

What is the most common kind of animal on Earth?

There are more than 350,000 species of beetles on Earth! That's about one-quarter of all the animals on the planet. They come in many shapes and sizes, from the pretty ladybug to the horned stag beetle.

horned stag beetle

ladybugs

BONUS TRIVIA

In many parts of the world, ladybugs are called ladybird beetles.

What is the biggest insect?

The giant weta is the largest and heaviest **insect** in the world. This cricket-like insect weighs about 2.5 ounces (70 g), which is heavier than a sparrow! Giant wetas are found only on a small island in New Zealand.

The giant weta is so big it can eat a carrot!

How are dust mites different from their spider cousins?

Dust mites and spiders are arachnids. They have eight legs and a hard outer skeleton. However, unlike spiders, dust mites don't have eyes, feelers, or even a head! They just have mouthparts, which they use to eat the skin flakes people shed.

How do jewel wasps keep food fresh for their young?

After a jewel wasp catches a cockroach, it **injects** a **chemical** into the roach's brain. The chemical stops the roach from wanting to move. The wasp then lays an egg on the roach. Once it hatches, the baby wasp begins eating the roach alive!

BONUS TRIVIA

This method keeps the cockroach alive for 7 or 8 days while the young wasp feeds.

jewel wasp

SMALL SEA LIFE

What are the loudest animals in the sea?

Beluga whales and sperm whales make very loud noises, but those giants have some pretty tiny **competition**. Snapping shrimp have a normal claw and a huge claw. They make a snapping sound that's louder than a gunshot with the larger claw.

Snapping shrimp only grow to about 2 inches (5 cm) long. However, a large group of snapping shrimp can be very loud!

The blue-ringed octopus normally looks brown all over. The blue rings appear when the octopus senses trouble.

BONUS TRIVIA

What is the deadliest animal in the sea?

The blue-ringed octopus might be small and cute, but it's also deadly. A single bite from this creature contains enough **venom** to kill a person in just minutes. Also, there are no drugs to treat the bite yet.

FREAKY FROGS!

Which animal spends winter frozen solid and thaws out in spring?

The wood frog doesn't travel south for winter. It doesn't **hibernate** in a warm cave. Instead, the wood frog hides under leaves on top of the ground. As temperatures drop, the frog freezes solid. In spring, it thaws out!

Wood frogs can be found throughout Canada and the northwest United States, and in Alaska.

How did the poison dart frog get its name?

Poison dart frogs are tiny, colorful animals from South America. They look cool, but they're very poisonous! The golden poison dart frog is so dangerous that native people used to make poison darts by rubbing the tips of the darts on the frog's back.

BONUS TRIVIA

The golden poison dart frog's body contains enough poison to kill 10 grown men.

FOR THE BIRDS

What is the fastest bird in the world?

Although some types of swifts can fly about 106 miles (171 km) per hour while flapping their wings, they're no match for a diving peregrine falcon. While zipping down to catch a meal, these birds can reach about 200 miles (322 km) per hour!

Peregrine falcons also have excellent eyesight, sharp talons, and a sharp beak. They're deadly hunters.

BONUS TRIVIA

What is the highest-flying bird?

Ruppell's griffon vulture, found in Africa, is a **soaring** bird. It drifts on warm air currents high in the sky as it searches for food. It's been spotted soaring more than 37,000 feet (11 km) above Earth's surface.

Ruppell's griffon vulture

What is the smallest bird?

The bee hummingbird of Cuba is the smallest bird in the world. It's about 2 inches (5 cm) long from the tip of its bill to the tip of its tail. This tiny bird weighs just 0.07 ounce (2 g), which is about the same as two dimes.

BONUS TRIVIA

The bee hummingbird flaps its wings between 50 and 80 times a second.

Male great bustards can grow up to 41 inches (104 cm) tall.

What is the heaviest flying bird?

Many people know that the flightless ostrich is the largest and heaviest bird in the world. However, the heaviest flying bird is the great bustard. Male great bustards can weigh up to 35 pounds (16 kg).

CHOMP!

Which animal has the most teeth?

Alligators? Nope. Sharks? Wrong again. The correct answer is snails! Some snail species have thousands of tiny teeth lined up in rows. These are what they use to munch holes in all the leafy vegetables in your garden.

BONUS TRIVIA

A snail's tiny teeth are called radulae (RA-juh-lee). They're perfect for tearing up soft plant parts.

Beavers use their teeth to gnaw on trees for food. They can even chop a tree down with their teeth!

Why are a beaver's teeth orange?

Beavers are well known for their strong teeth. They should be strong—their outer surface has iron in it! Most animals have teeth made of the element calcium, but iron is stronger. It's the iron that makes beaver teeth orange.

THAT'S LIFE!

Which animal might live forever?

A species of Mediterranean jellyfish discovered in 1883 might be **immortal**. When in danger, the jellyfish attaches itself to something and changes into a blob. The blob then changes into a young jellyfish. By doing this, this jellyfish could possibly live forever!

The immortal jellyfish is about 0.19 inch (5 mm) long.

Adult mayflies can't eat because their mouthparts don't move.

Which animal has the shortest adult life span?

There are about 2,000 mayfly species. Mayflies are babies—called nymphs—for 2 weeks to 2 years, depending on the species. Once they become adults, however, the longest they live is about 2 days. Some species live just a few hours!

BONUS TRIVIA

Mayflies are members of the scientific group Ephemeroptera (eh-feh-muh-RAHP-tuh-ruh). This name comes from the Greek words for "short-lived" and "wing."

ANIMALS IN SPACE?

Other than people, what animals have traveled into outer space?

In 1957, a Russian dog named Laika became the first animal to circle Earth in a spacecraft. Since then, many other animals have been in outer space, including monkeys, chimpanzees, mice, rats, guinea pigs, cats, turtles, rabbits, fish, jellyfish, frogs, insects, spiders, and worms.

Laika

Challenge Yourself

You've learned many awesome trivia facts about animals, but why stop there? What's the world's smallest animal? What's the smelliest? Which animal lays the most eggs at one time? Keep exploring the animal kingdom to build up your trivia knowledge.

GLOSSARY

blood vessel: a small tube in an animal's body that carries blood

chemical: matter that can be mixed with other matter to cause changes

competition: a struggle to be better than others at something

hibernate: to be in a sleeplike state for an extended period of time, usually during winter

immortal: never dying

inject: to use sharp teeth to force venom into an animal's body

insect: a small, often winged, animal with six legs and three body parts

savanna: a grassland with scattered patches of trees

soar: to drift in the air without flapping wings

spine: a long, sharp body part

venom: something an animal makes in its body that can harm other animals

FOR MORE INFORMATION

Books

National Geographic. *Ultimate Weird but True*. Washington, DC: National Geographic, 2011.

Peterson, Megan Cooley. *This Book Might Bite: A Collection of Wacky Animal Trivia*. North Mankato, MN: Capstone Press, 2012.

Seuling, Barbara. *Cows Sweat Through Their Noses: And Other Freaky Facts About Animal Habits, Characteristics, and Homes*. Minneapolis, MN: Picture Window Books, 2008.

Websites

Animal Classes
www.kidzone.ws/animals/animal_classes.htm
Learn more about the many different types of animals on Earth.

National Geographic Kids
kids.nationalgeographic.com/kids/
This website is a great place to learn interesting facts about any animal you can think of.

INDEX